I0468601

# Beginners Drawing Book

## Learn to draw human figures

by Rebecca Cooper

# Table of Contents

# Disclaimer

While all attempts have been made to verify the information provided in this book, the author does assume any responsibility for errors, omissions, or contrary interpretations of the subject matter contained within. **The information provided in this book is for educational and entertainment purposes only. The reader is responsible for his or her own actions and the author does not accept any responsibilities for any liabilities or damages, real or perceived, resulting from the use of this information.**

The trademarks that are used are without any consent, and the publication of the trademark is without permission or backing by the trademark owner. All trademarks and brands within this book are for clarifying purposes only and are the owned by the owners themselves, not affiliated with this document.

# Introduction

Girl simply beginning are regularly baffled by the subject of how to draw girl. The type of a man wearing garments can be really mind boggling and this goes considerably more for the human body itself.

How about we expect you stay there with a charcoal and an unfilled sheet of drawing paper before you - and also a figure of a human with dress. Next, you ponder, where do I begin for the love of all that is holy? How would I start? Taking a look at the figure, the errand can appear to be entirely overwhelming.

In this way, how about we begin with a fundamental rule. Any drawing can be taken back to a couple of segments. On account of a human figure, the body can be partitioned into a few sections. Simply solicit yourself, where might the center from the body be? The answer is straightforward: at the waistline.

It's essential to get the fundamental extents right to begin with, and not to include subtle element to start with. Just If you are certain that the extents are about right, would you be able to include (just little) detail later. You can help that procedure considerably shutting your eyes when taking a look at your model. Along these lines, you concentrate on the expansive shapes and not on the subtle elements.

Next, you can do some fundamental measuring. Take your pencil, hold it vertically while your arm is at full length. At that point put your thumb where the feet are. Next, move the thumb position to the waistline without taking your thumb off the pencil. Check if the pencil's top is in accordance with the head's top. If that isn't the situation, then you ought to change the position until you locate the exact midpoint which is generally at waist stature. After every estimation, you ought to make a little check on your paper sheet as an essential rule.

The accompanying step is to attempt and measure the head from the button to the top. The body is around seven times bigger than the head.

Next, you will need to make a blemish on your drawing sheet to show where the base of the feet is.

How about we recap: you ought to now have a blemish on your drawing paper where the base of the feet, the waistline, the jaw and the highest point of the head are. Presently you can survey them and choose if the extents look alright. Look from your drawing to the figure and back once more. Do it entirely quick. You will check whether it the extents aren't precisely right. All things considered, transform them.

As I said, the whole head is around one seventh of the length of the body. These standards, coincidentally, ought to be utilized as an essential rule just, not any guideline that is cut in stone. Simply look from your drawing to the figure and back once more, and see what's there. That is the way to getting the right estimations.

Next, you can make marks for other key parts of the body. Obviously, there are the legs and arms. At the point when the arms are casual, the fingers are about five head down and the knees around six, so put marks there.

At full face, the width of the body is three heads wide. So make a line from the groin to the base where you have denoted the feet.

Along these lines, now you essentially know how to draw girl the key thing is to continue honing and you will show signs of improvement at it. Have a great time!

A noteworthy piece of learning to draw girl is about learning how to draw garments. So you have to give careful consideration to it. How garments stream and how they wrinkle depending on the fabric sort is vital for making a decent drawing. Remember that a three piece suite cresses uniquely in contrast to a plain vanilla cotton shirt.

Next most vital thing is extent of human figure. When you draw a full figure you must get this privilege. Any book on life systems for craftsmen will be a decent hotspot for learning about human body extents. While concentrating on extents remember that extents for male body are not the same as that of female body. What's more, notwithstanding that a youngster's body extents don't coordinate with an adult's.

Eyes, eye temples and mouth are the three regions that you will use to express the feelings your character is feeling. At the point when drawing eyes, remember that our eye surface is constantly soggy and reflects light. To make this impact include minimal white spots operating at a profit bit of eyes this will make your character all the more enthusiastic.

Drawing a decent human character involves more than drawing a biped animal; you're drawing ought to likewise pass on encompassing environment. Also, rise to cautious arranging is required here. If it is an indoor scene some furniture and different extras will make your character more acceptable. In the event that your character is outside a few trees may arrive in the edge.

Last words: Though a tips article like this single-handedly cannot show you how to make lovely drawings of girl the rules given in the article if took after will make your work less demanding to handle. To be capable you have to see the works of experts and comprehend their exceptional styles. Or more all go to field and make drawing of real girl. Drawing from different drawings or picture won't take you exceptionally far.

# Chapter 1 – How to draw girl 1

Step 1: Sketch a circle for the head and a little elliptical for the body.

Step 2: Sketch the rules for the face and in addition the button and the jaw line.

Step 3: Add the furthest points (face parts, eyes, nose, ears and so on).

Step 4: Sketch 2 hovers for the eyes.

Step 5: Sketch the hair's draft. It relies on upon you.

Step 6: Make sure that we are highlighting her hair in this drawing so, you have especially worked on shading her hair.

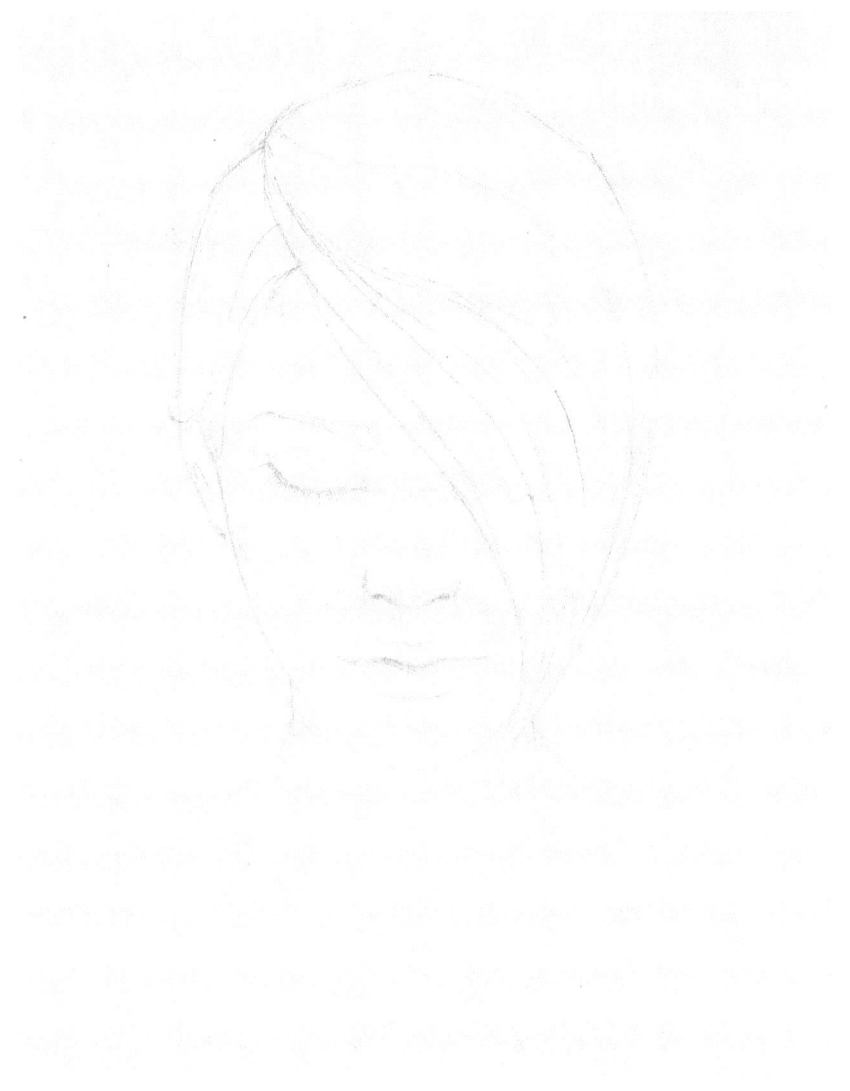

Step 7: Erase the draft and put in more points of interest.

Step 8: Sketch the fundamental parts which you need to highlight in the young lady.

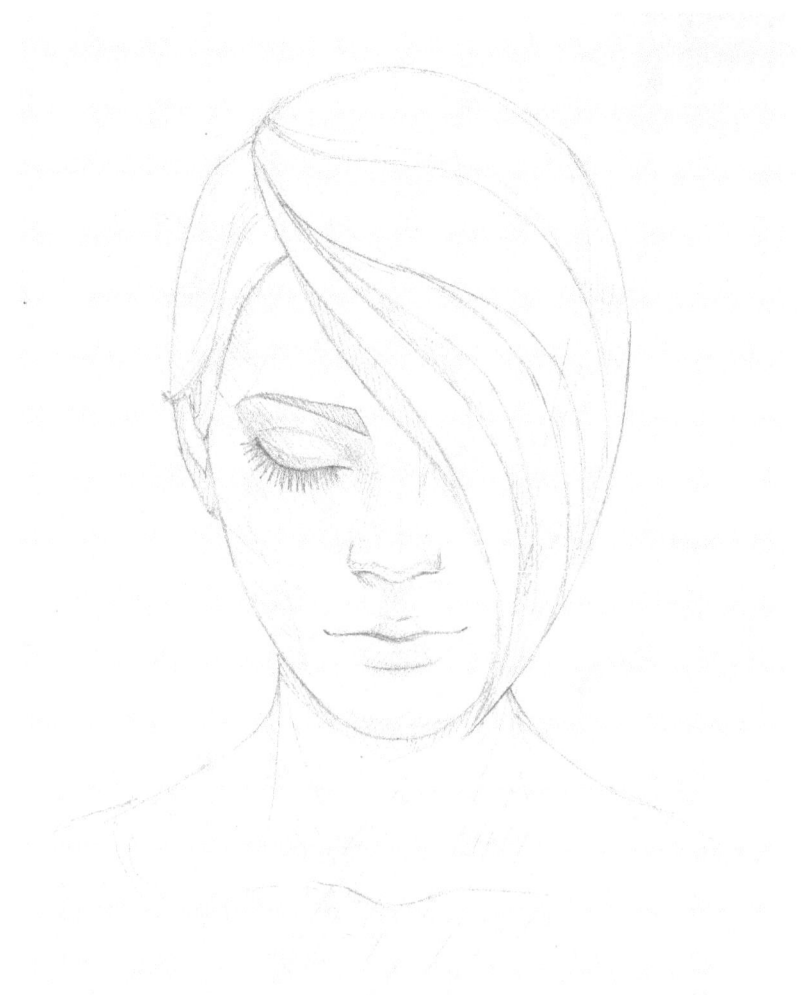

Step 9: Now you can see the girl is completed and we have sketched the parts which we wanted to highlight.

# Chapter 2 – How to draw girl 2

Step 1: Begin off by making the head and middle aides like along these lines, and then sketch in the facial rules.

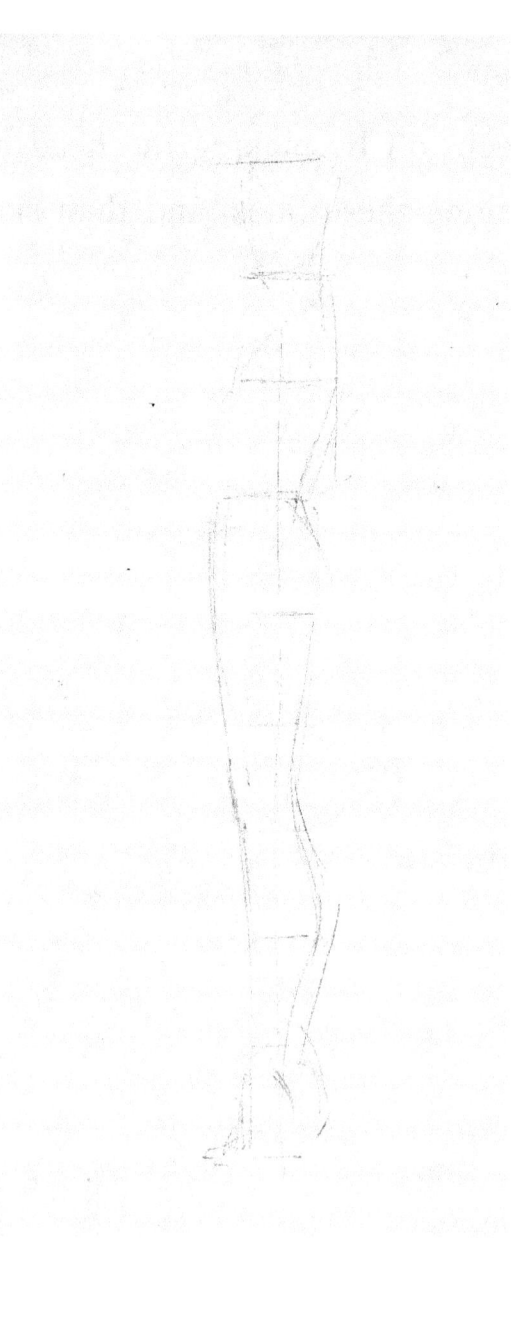

Step 2: In this stride you should simply draw out the right half of the face shape or covering like so. At the point when that is done you can start the drawing procedure for her hair which is uneven to the extent blasts go. You can likewise draw any haircut you like taking into account your inclination.

Step 3: In this stride you will keep on chipping away at the young lady's face shape and additionally her ear and the hair that falls in favor of her face simply over her ear. Include specifying within the ear, then continue to step four. But let's make sure that we are drawing this girl in a manner that she's standing.

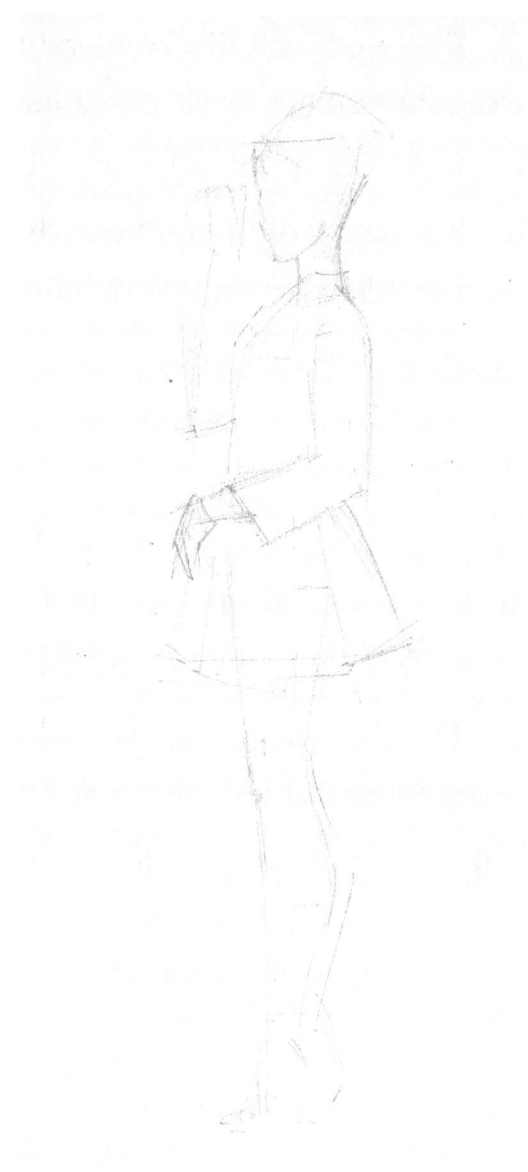

Step 4: Since a face's portion is done, you can start taking a shot at the eyes. Begin with the long upper eyelid, then draw and shading in the eyeball like you

see here. We are drawing from the side and her skirt is above her knees.


Step 5: Make sure that we draw her shades on her face as we know that she's standing.

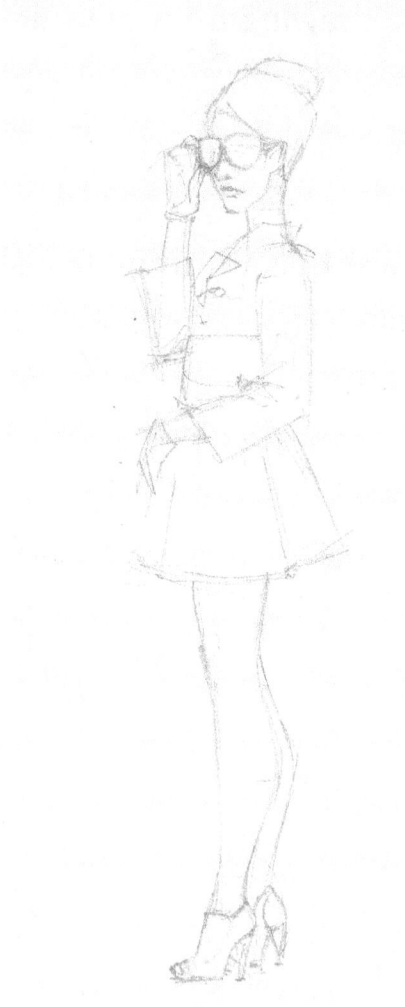

Step 6: Rather on of proceeding with the body, we will wrap up her long straight hair. I like how her hair is somewhat harsh or shaggy looking on the grounds that it makes her look considerably more sweltering.

When you wrap up the hair, you can continue to step seven.

Step 7: All you need to do here is draw her hair in such a way that the main attraction is her hair. As they are in the bow.

Step 8: How about we begin drawing the body starting with the middle, stomach and thigh. You will likewise need to draw the arm which is covered up in favor of her body.

Step 9: For the last drawing step you should simply draw the waist bands, then draw the crease and pocket line. Add enumerating to her back like in this way, and then delete the oversights.

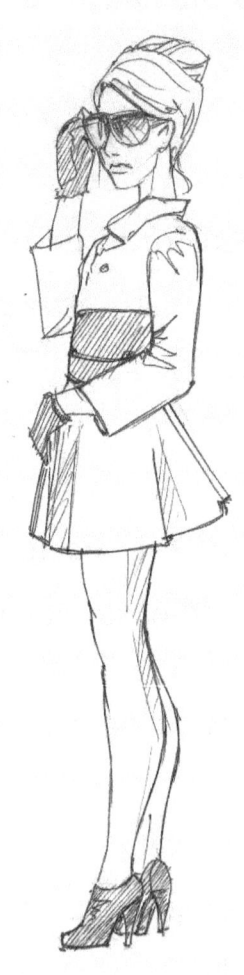

Step 10: That is it, you are done and this is the manner by which your young lady looks when wrapped up. Everything you need to do now is shading her in.

# Chapter 3 – How to draw girl 3

Step 1: Sketch the head. Draw a circle and a bended line under that for the button. Add rules like those appeared to help you with the facial elements.

Step 2: Add two circles for the eyes and two dainty bended lines over that for the eyebrows. Draw two half-hovers for the ears, on the same rule as the eyes.

Step 3: Add a little nose and modest pair of lips. They can be bigger or

look changed, on the other hand, in the event that you need a less cartoonish or charming looking young lady.

Step 4: Sketch in the hair. Draw blasts for her and make her hair short, or keep it long and wavy. Utilize your creative energy.

Step 5: Now sketch in the body. Draw a little neck for her, a circle for the abdominal area and an oval for the lower body.

Step 6: Add last lines and any extra points of interest, as eyelashes, strips, and so forth. The specifics are dependent upon you- - once more, be inventive!

Step 7: Outline the young lady and eradicate the rules. You can likewise include some kind of

foundation or another outside component to your drawing as of right now, for example, shadowing.

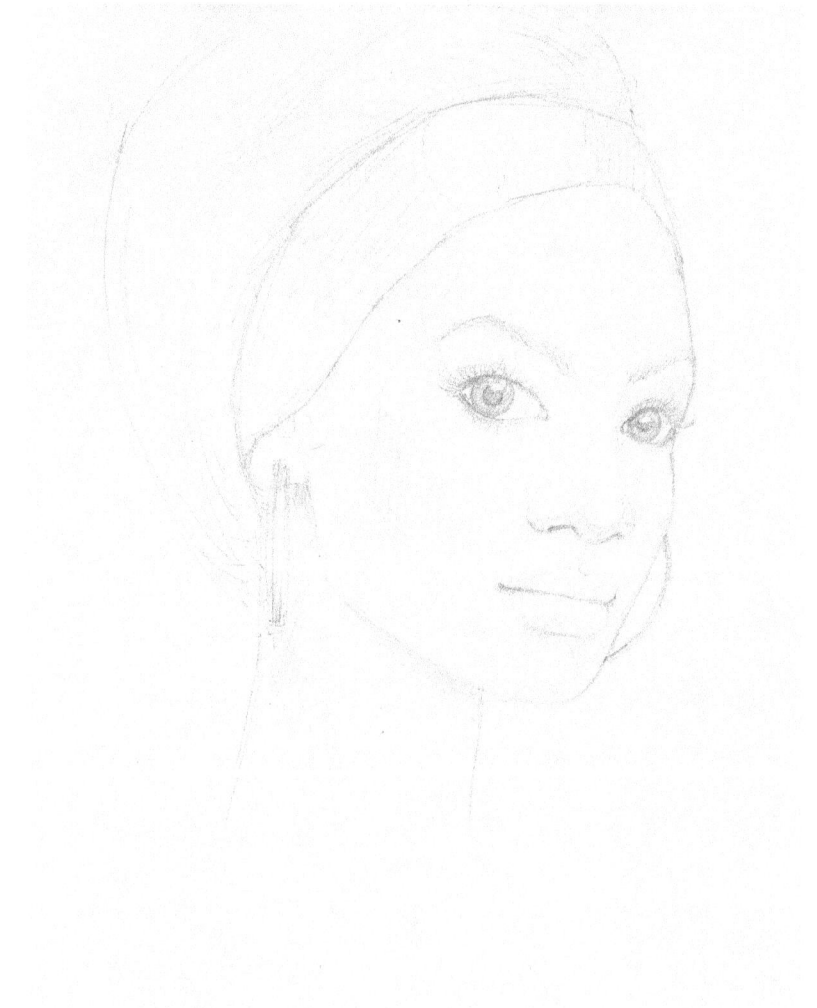

Step 8: Sketch the parts you want to highlight in the girl, such as her shoes.

# Chapter 4 – How to draw girl 4

Step 1: Begin with a circle for the head and after that draw a center line for the focal point of the body posture.

Step 2: Draw the state of her face, and after that start drawing out her beautiful haircut beginning with the front hair line.

Step 3: Draw thick top eyelids like you see here and make a point to have the lashes flare at the finishes for the lashes. Next, draw the slight eyebrow lines and afterward make an ear shape and also her smile.

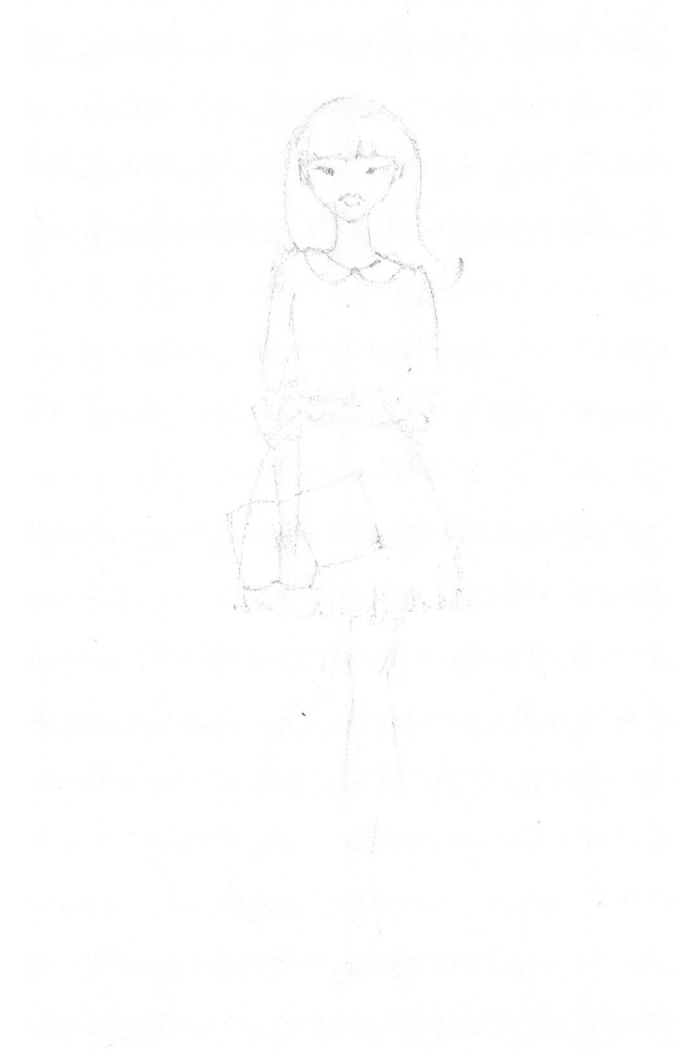

Step 4: Complete the process of adding so as to draw out the eyes the eyeballs. As should be obvious the left half of the eye is thick. Sketch the redden

blemishes on her cheeks, and afterward include the ear specifying.

Step 5: Just draw out her full looking haircut which is long and kind of wavy.

Step 6: Presently you can get occupied by taking a shot at getting her body drawn out. You can do this by drawing the shoulders, and after that her stout style arms and hands like so.

Step 7: Draw her hair as if they are good in length.

Step 8: Keep on drawing out her dress, and after that draw the lap. As should be obvious her end line of the dress is wavy, so make certain to do likewise and in addition sketch in a few wrinkles and overlap.

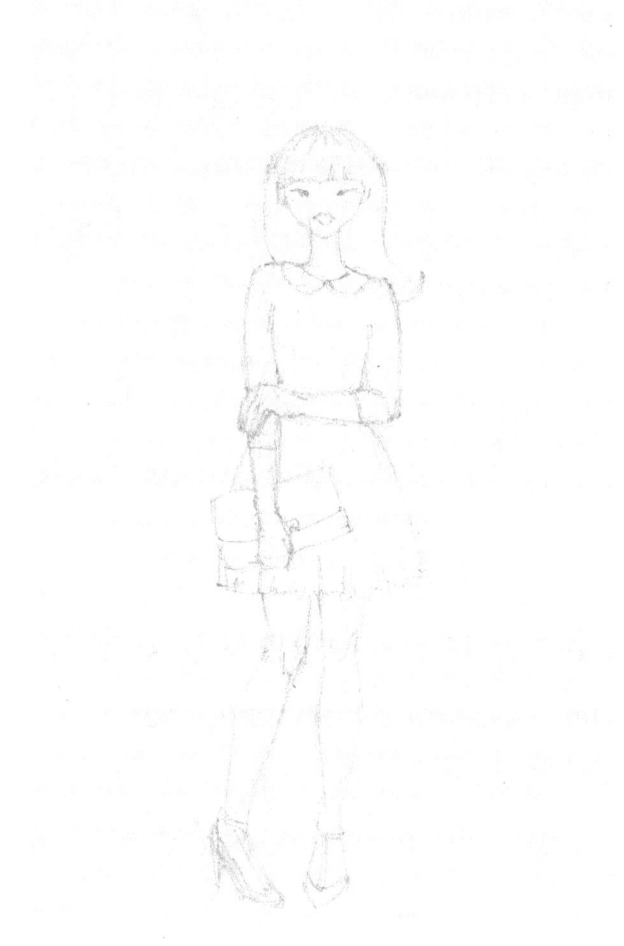

Step 9: Draw the dress' base under her butt, and after that sketch out the state of the thick style legs and feet and also the little heels.

Step 10: Draw her hair short and cute, make sure that her skirt has frills so for that we will shade the shirt in with dark black pen as well as her heels.

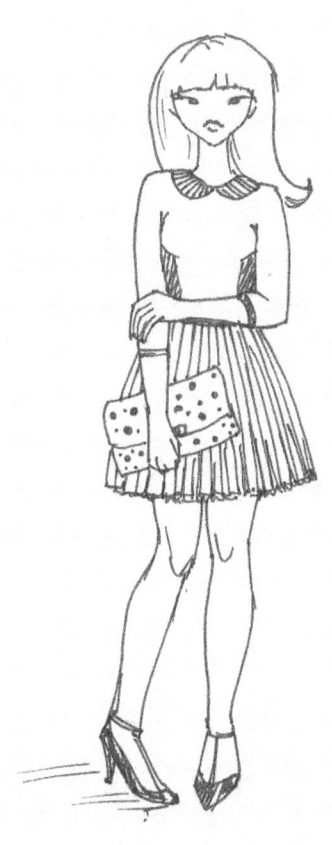

Step 11: Shade the hang bad that she has in her hands, as well as her t-shirt that we have shown in her figure.

# Chapter 5 – How to draw girl 5

Step 1: the head. This is likely a standout amongst the most troublesome parts, on the grounds that it is so difficult to make symmetrical, however once you get accustomed to it's a great deal simpler. So include the ears, and you're prepared for step two.

Step 2:  the hair. This is one of my extremely most loved parts. Simply choose which heading you need the hair to go, and after that simply draw it. You can simply do it another way, and If you need it wavy, there are more.

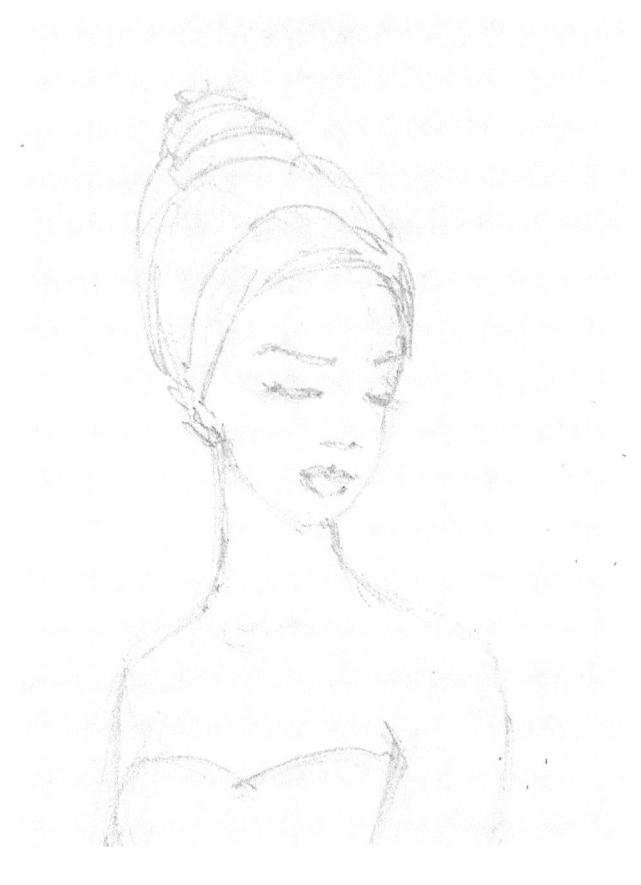

Step 3: Simply make a point to draw a characterizing line where the hair comes over the face, If it does, and that likewise helps separate the once more from the hair's front.

Step 6: Now we can work on the face outlines such as her eye-brows, lips, ears with earrings and nose.

Step 7: Make sure that we have drawn a bun in her hair to show the attractiveness of it. And also the necklace should be drawn with the necklace.

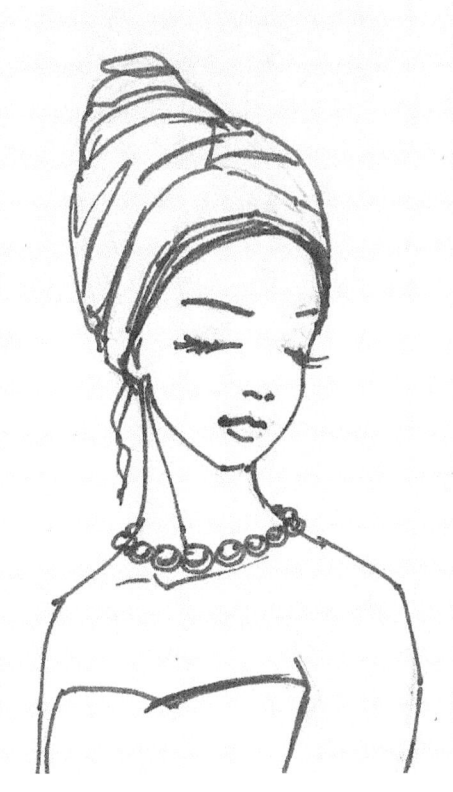

Step 8: Simply include the shading and you're up and running! Bear in mind, you can change any angle to make this photo your own. Have some good times, and please remark!

# Chapter 6 – How to draw girl 6

Step 1: In the first place, we require a few rules. Draw 8 areas rise to long.

Step 2: Draw an oval that takes up one segment of the eight. The oval ought to be somewhat more than it is wide. Next draw two lines for a neck. And then draw her hair with the little hat that she's wearing as in the figure.

Step 3: Draw two circles for the shoulders. The figure is turned somewhat, so the circle on the privilege ought to be a touch more remote than adjusted to the right half of the head. The left circle ought to be adjusted to one side of the head.

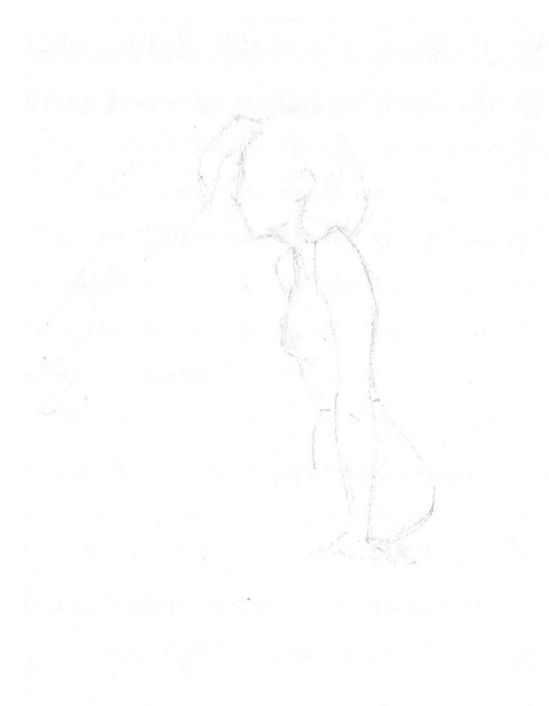

Step 4: Develop the left's bend circle to about the same separation as the circle's edge. Draw her breasts as we can see the cleavage of her as in the pic.

Step 5: Get the line down a tender outward bend to the third's end area. Presently draw a bending line from the left edge of the right circle. Begin the bend as an outward bend, and afterward transform it to an internal bend.

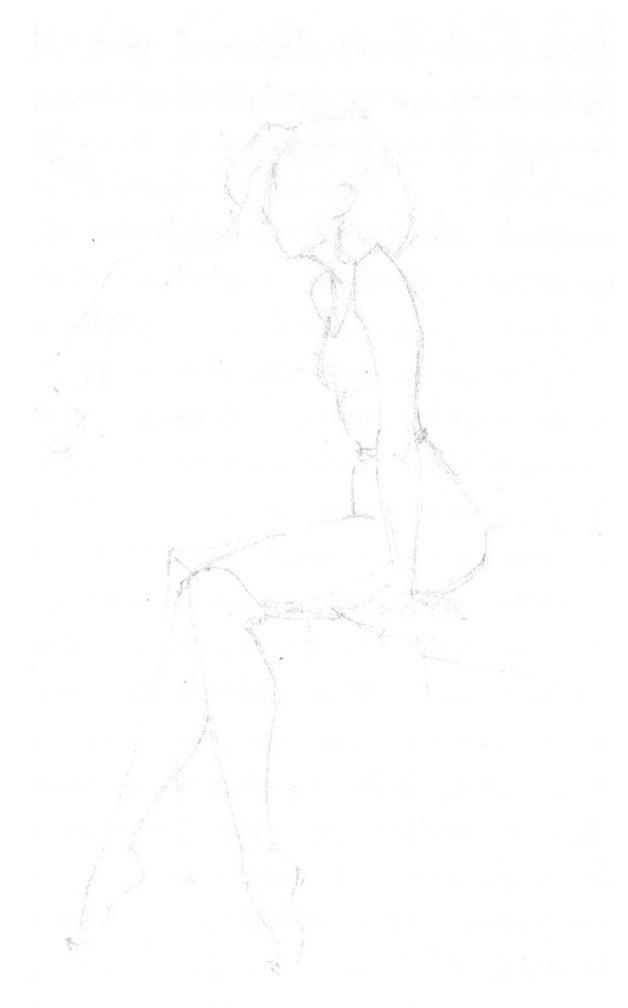

Step 6: The scarf is flowing away with the wind, so make sure that toy draw it like that.

Step 7: Time for the legs! Design drawing legs are long, so make the thighs broaden one and a half segments.

Step 8: Draw some long ovals that go somewhat more than the part of the way through the last segment. Presently modify the legs' state. Bend the inward

sides of the legs, making the bends' tops on the higher side.

Step 9: You can shading, shade, and complete it any way you like.

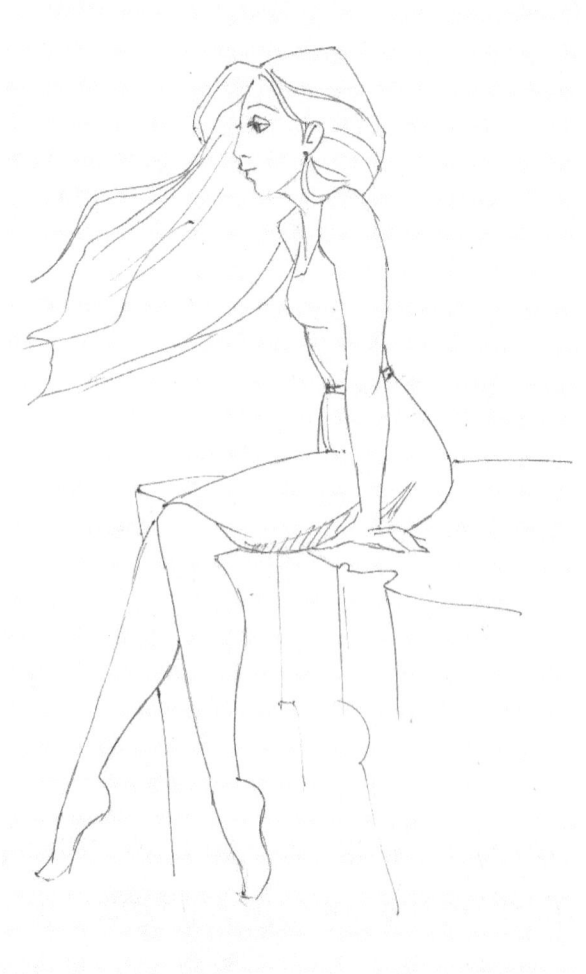

Step 10: Sketch the parts that need to be highlighted.

# Chapter 7: How to draw girl 7

Step 1: Draw the head in a moderate movement.

Step 2: Circulate the head with a knock. If you commit an error, eradicate it with the eraser.

Step 3: Draw the neck wavy. As well as show her hand with a flower.

Step 4: Put a line amidst the base end.

Step 5: Put the hair in a bun, and show some flowers.

Step 6: Draw her hair in a dark manner with the flora.

Step 7: Then draw a flower on her hair.

Step 8: Draw two flowers then and shade them.

Step 9: Draw the lips dark and clean.

Step 10: Then, put on her clothes with a cleavage neck.

Step 11: Draw a light flora pattern on her cloths as well.

Step 12: Sketch her hair entirely with the dark shading in it.

Step 13: Draw her hair pattern as she's wearing something on her head.

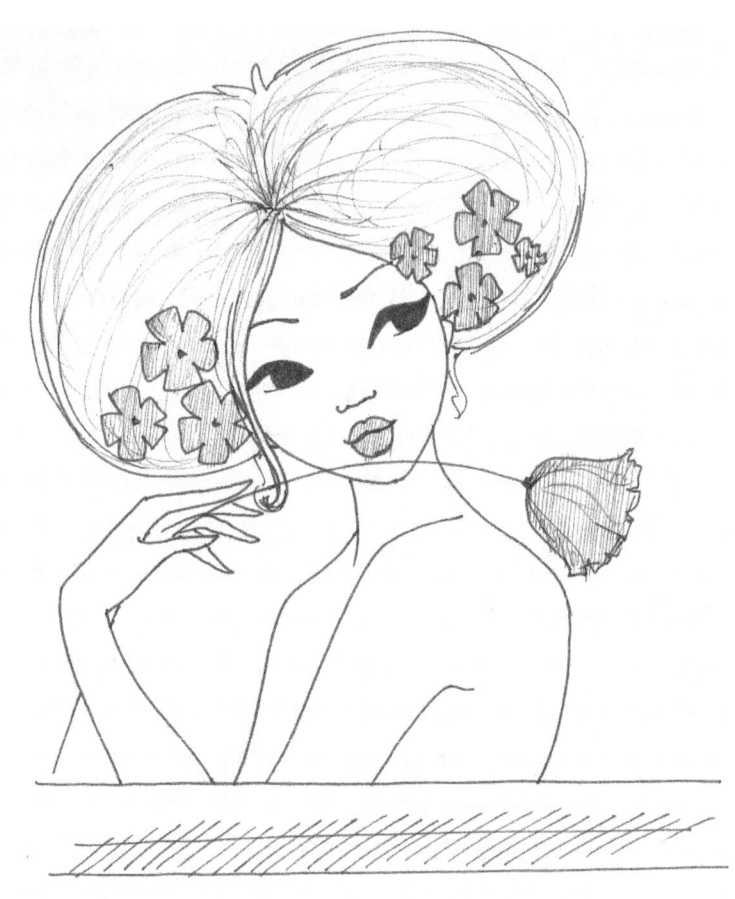

Step 14: Draw the pattern with dark shading as well.

Step 15: Sketch wherever necessary.

# Conclusion

It's just regular that as girl, most craftsmen need to have the capacity to know how to draw girl. It's a helpful expertise to have, too, as having the capacity to sketch out a photo of a companion or cherished one makes for an extraordinary blessing.

An extraordinary spot to begin when learning how to draw girl is the head. Begin with some sketched circles, it doesn't need to be great. You'll be driving the facial components at the lower a portion of the front, yet a fundamental circle will give respectable system. Since you have your circle, draw a vertical and level line through and through and side to side, yet stop for a minute.

Attempt to think of your head as being three dimensional and marginally confronting down and to one side or left. Presently without looking straight on, however more off kilter a bit, envision where the eyes, mouth, and nose would be and draw the lines between the eyes for the vertical, and simply over the mouth and beneath the nose. You can think of the head as to a greater extent a globe in these early stages. When you have those two confining lines revolving around your globe, you can work in the eyes, nose, mouth, the majority of the fundamental facial components truly. It's a great deal simpler once you have a reference point.

Moving alongside how to draw girl and down the structure, we can go to the neck. Keep in mind the neck in the back is to a great extent a continuation of the head, though in the front of the head it the jaw cuts in possibly 33% of the route before descending. Turn out to start to frame the shoulders. Try not to stress a lot over muscle definition or anything towards that end yet. You can sketch in some conditioning lines here or there, yet you can include the greater part later, at this moment we're simply worried with getting the fundamental structure together.

The following stride in how to draw girl secured will be the mid-section. You can utilize another three dimensional circle as you accomplished for the head here too. The top side regions of the circle where it bends off can be utilized as a premise for setting the arm pits, and from that point you can fill in the arms and unite them to the shoulders. Utilize the same thought for the vertical line to separate the mid-section and ribcage.

Completing up the lesson on the most proficient method to draw girl, it's really clear from here on. It's to a great extent up to you as to where you need to start to move from the mid-section/stomach into the legs as far as how far you need to extend and how high up you'll do it. Verify you turn out fairly to make it more sensible and make tracks in an opposite direction from the picture of the stick man. The knee joints will have a little definition, and the calves will turn out a bit, too, before narrowing out again and closure with the feet. Since you have the essential structure down, you can include more elements, definition, tone, and muscle and bone structure by including imprints here and there. Sketched can go far.

I built up my adoration for drawing when I was first ready to hold a pencil at 4 years old. The first occasion when I had the capacity convey life to a clear white bit of paper I was dependent. As I became more seasoned and the obligations of life started to mount I lost the flexibility to express my innovative gifts all the time and my craft ability languished over it. One day I looked in the mirror and understood that what I cherished doing the most was an inconsequential piece of my day by day life.

I want to draw figures and find penciling a magnum opus of human life systems a thrilling background. I chose to quick track my training process and contract a private teacher. Following one month of direction I had gained some ground yet my wallet couldn't stay aware of the expenses included.

This is the point at which I understood the web is the ideal spot for me to discover the data required to learn how to draw girl and figures the right way. After a huge amount of examination online I at long last discovered a system called Figure Drawing Secrets that has empowered me to accomplish my objective!